Let It Be

Let It Be

Advent and Christmas Meditations for Women

Edited by
Therese Johnson Borchard

A Crossroad Book
The Crossroad Publishing Company
New York

The Crossroad Publishing Company
370 Lexington Avenue, New York, NY 10017

Printed in the United States of America

Library of Congress Cataloging-in-Publication Data

Let it be : Advent and Christmas meditations for women / edited by Therese Johnson
Borchard.
    p.   cm.
  ISBN 0-8245-1767-9 (pbk.)
    1. Women—Prayer-books and devotions—English. 2. Advent—Prayer-books
and devotions—English. 3. Christmas—Prayer-books and devotions—English.
4. Epiphany—Prayer-books and devotions—English.   I. Borchard, Therese
Johnson.
BV4844.L47   1998   98-18349
242'. 643—dc21   CIP

1 2 3 4 5 6 7 8 9 10 03 02 01 00 99 98

*I dedicate this book
to my sister Sarah,
who is pregnant
with her first child.*

Contents

PREFACE

In the sixth month the angel Gabriel was sent by God to a town in Galilee called Nazareth, to a virgin engaged to a man whose name was Joseph, of the house of David. The virgin's name was Mary.

And he came to her and said, "Greetings, favored one! The Lord is with you." But she was much perplexed by his words and pondered what sort of greeting this might be.

The angel said to her, "Do not be afraid, Mary, for you have found favor with God. And now, you will conceive in your womb and bear a son, and you will name him Jesus. He will be great, and will be called the Son of the Most High, and the Lord God will give to him the throne of his ancestor David. He will reign over the house of Jacob forever, and of his kingdom there will be no end."

Mary said to the angel, "How can this be, since I am a virgin?"

The angel said to her, "The Holy Spirit will come upon you, and the power of the Most High will overshadow you; therefore the child to be born will be holy; he will be called Son of God.

*And now, your relative Elizabeth in her old age
has also conceived a son; and this is the sixth
month for her who was said to be barren. For
nothing will be impossible with God."*

*Then Mary said, "Here am I, the servant of
the Lord; let it be with me according to your
word."*

—Luke 1:26-38

Mary's yes to life is our beginning. The holy moment that she responds to the angel Gabriel, "Let it be with me according to your word," is the commencement of our intimacy with God. The fiat proclaimed by the Mother of God begins the Incarnation—God made human—and initiates our Christian story of redemption; by agreeing to participate fully in life and in salvation history, Mary inaugurates the Paschal Mystery.

We learn from Mary's example of faith and trust in God. Although she does not fully understand what is to happen to her, she allows it, and asks God to grant her the knowledge and wisdom as she needs it. Her simple response to the angel forever echoes perfect faith and trust in God.

In her book *Mary: Shadow of Grace*, Megan McKenna offers us a beautiful description of the woman first known as Miriam of Nazareth.

Mary is a believer, not a knower. She
believes in her child, and through crises and
events she seeks meaning and insight, the gifts
of wisdom and understanding and knowledge.

She is a silent, reflective woman, seeking to
understand and know her God and her child and

God's will for her life day to day. She treasures
words, events, moments in her life as revealing
to her the power and might of God, as
incarnating the presence of God as father and
Lord of her life. Simple, ordinary human
occurrences are her path to knowledge. She
experiences conversion, insight, and ever-
deepening awareness and love of God by the
way God deals with her, in her present reality.

We know so few words from Mary's mouth:
only the poetry of "let it be done to me according
to your Word," the stanzas of the Magnificat.
Her other voices are memory and silence. Her
mind and heart grow words of surrender,
obedience, and belief—words on behalf of
others, in witness to others' pain and desperate
hope.

This compilation is meant to be a prayer guide through
each day of Advent, from the first Sunday of Advent to the
Feast of the Epiphany. In it, I have included many of the
great women spiritual writers of our day so to invite readers
to journey with them toward the joyous feast of Christmas
and onward to the light of the Epiphany. Each entry of the
companion presents a theme beginning with a scripture
passage from the lectionary readings of the day, following
with a selection of text from a popular woman author, and
concluding with a prayer.

I offer this companion as a way to gather women together during this holy season of Advent and Christmas so
that we may learn from each other, and celebrate together the
intimate birth of our Lord into the world. As women of faith
we look to Mary for the courage to say yes to God in our
lives, for the willingness to be instruments of divine love,

and for the humility to participate fully in life according to
God's plan. With the Mother of the Word, women join
together at Christmas to sing Mary's song of joy:

> *My soul magnifies the Lord,*
> *and my spirit rejoices in God my Savior,*
> *for he has looked with favor on the lowliness of*
> *his servant.*
> *Surely, from now on all generations will call*
> *me blessed;*
> *for the Mighty One has done great things for me,*
> *and holy is his name.*
> *His mercy is for those who fear him*
> *from generation to generation.*
> *He has shown strength with his arm;*
> *he has scattered the proud in the thoughts of*
> *their hearts.*
> *He has brought down the powerful from their*
> *thrones,*
> *and lifted up the lowly;*
> *he has filled the hungry with good things,*
> *and sent the rich away empty.*
> *He has helped his servant Israel,*
> *in remembrance of his mercy,*
> *according to the promise he made to our*
> *ancestors,*
> *to Abraham and to his descendants forever.*

—Luke 1:46-55

THANKS

I'd like to thank all of my friends at Crossroad for
their help developing and producing this and other
books: Matthew Laughlin, Bob Byrns, Lynn Quinn,
Providence Calderon, Vanessa Wong, Juan Alvarado,
and others. I want to extend a special thanks to Mike
Leach and Gwendolin Herder, the great minds
behind this and many of Crossroad's publications.

WATCH AND PRAY

Mark 13:33-37

*Beware, keep alert; for you do not know when
the time will come. It is like a man going on a
journey, when he leaves home and puts his slaves
in charge, each with his work, and commands
the doorkeeper to be on the watch. Therefore,
keep awake—for you do not know when the
master of the house will come, in the evening, or
at midnight, or at cockcrow, or at dawn, or else
he may find you asleep when he comes suddenly.
And what I say to you I say to all: Keep awake.*

One of the words people use frequently about prayer is
intercession. . . . To intercede means being a bridge on which
God and a particular person, a group of people, or a certain
situation meet. In other words, it means burden-bearing on
behalf of others. Just as four men carried their paralyzed
friend to Jesus in the hope that Jesus would heal him, so we
carry people and situations to God trusting that he will
intervene on their behalf. Intercession is therefore a costly,
selfless way of loving people and the world.

When we take seriously [Jesus'] challenge to pray with
humility, the nature of our intercessory prayer may well
change. Some people spend a great deal of time describing a
problem or crisis to God as though he, the all-seeing One,
knows nothing of the situation about which we feel so

deeply. They then proceed to tell him how to solve the
problem as though they have forgotten that he is all-wise as
well as all-powerful. In his graciousness and generosity, God
hears these prayers but he gently calls us into a more costly,
more authentic way of interceding.

He convinces us that, since he started praying for the
people or situation long before we did and since he is far
wiser than we are, our responsibility is to seek to discover
the nature of his prayer and to echo it rather than to counter-
act his prayer with our own requests. He shows us that this
inevitably means listening and waiting rather than
clamouring and dictating—that we need him to interpret the
feebleness of our prayer. When we echo the prayer of Jesus,
we find that we pray, not from our lips only, but from our
hearts. In fact we may quickly come to the place where we
run out of words and we weep or groan or, more conscious
of God's greatness than the enormity of the problem, we
simply hold a person or a crisis into his love.

—Joyce Huggett, *Learning the Language of Prayer*

Prayer

I come before you, Lord,
    holding my intentions near.
Let my prayer be as an echo of your love,
    filled with holy silence and stillness,
    and the sounds of your peace.
Teach me to listen and wait as I pray,
    so that I may know and understand
    your prayer to me.
Amen.

CLIMB THE MOUNTAIN

Isaiah 2:2-3

In days to come
    the mountain of the Lord's house
shall be established as the highest of the
        mountains,
    and shall be raised above the hills;
all the nations shall stream to it.
    Many peoples shall come and say,
"Come, let us go up to the mountain of
        the Lord,
    to the house of the God of Jacob;
that he may teach us his ways
    and that we may walk in his paths."
For out of Zion shall go forth instruction,
    and the word of the Lord from Jerusalem.

When I first began hiking in the Rocky Mountains, I was on a trail I'd not traveled before. It led to a spectacular lake surrounded by cliffs. It was not a particularly difficult path, but I was not used to the altitude and my midlife body was doing a lot of huffing and puffing. I had stopped to rest at a place where I needed to climb over some boulders in order to continue upward. I had no idea of how much farther I had to walk, but I was getting weary and worn out.

Just then, a family came bounding down the path. In the lead was a small girl about six years old, long blond hair swinging in the breeze. She was as alive and alert as I was winded and half-dead. She stopped when she reached me, looked at me with great compassion and exclaimed, "It's not much further. It's really worth it. You're almost there!"

I will never forget those words. They echoed in my spirit the rest of that day and far beyond. They reminded me of how much I need others to help keep my dreams alive. I also heard those words as the voice of my divine companion, encouraging me and promising me that the midlife journey to my true Self would be well worth the effort. It truly has been.

—Joyce Rupp, *Dear Heart, Come Home*

Prayer

Great is the Lord and greatly to be praised
in the city of our God.
His holy mountain, beautiful in elevation,
is the joy of all the earth,
Mount Zion, in the far north,
the city of the great King.
Within its citadels God
has shown himself a sure defense.

Walk about Zion, go all around it,
count its towers,
consider well its ramparts;
go through its citadels,
that you may tell the next generation
that this is God,
our God forever and ever.
He will be our guide forever.

—*Psalm 48:1-3, 12-14*

BECOME LIKE CHILDREN

Luke 10:21, 23

Jesus rejoiced in the Holy Spirit and said, "I thank you, Father, Lord of heaven and earth, because you have hidden these things from the wise and the intelligent and have revealed them to infants; yes, Father, for such was your gracious will."

Then turning to the disciples, Jesus said to them privately, "Blessed are the eyes that see what you see! For I tell you that many prophets and kings desired to see what you see, but did not see it, and to hear what you hear, but did not hear it."

Through the willingness to be vastly, desperately ignorant, we become receptive to sudden inspired wisdom. First we are willing to be powerless, then we become more sincere; then God comes. "Except ye become as little children, ye shall never enter the kingdom of heaven." They forgot to mention that it is the children who would make plain our powerlessness to us.

Our native desire for love leads us toward God. It manifests itself as a desire to trust. Where we let our children down and are forced to admit that on our own we cannot fail to fail, there comes again this cry for something to trust. We find many ways to deny or sedate this urge, but then along come our children *trusting us!* Oh, God.

20

Why bring God into this? Why complicate things? We've got each other—what more is there? But whether you call it Higher Power or Order of Being or Fundamental Mind or One Mind or Our Father or Our Mother or Life, the fact is that God is the only truly simplifying factor. It is trying to live without God that is so complicated and hard. Having children, having each other, may not be turning out to be as terrific as we imagined. Somehow someone is always feeling had. Jesus saw this. He said, "A man's foes will be those of his own household" (Matthew 10:36).

So, loving them, we grow. Partly we want so badly for it to be good for them, to renovate our own childhoods, and to prove ourselves to our parents (actual or at large, interior or exterior, dead, alive, or imaginary). Also, we don't want to let this opportunity of family life drift by just coping and hanging in there without receiving the blessing we know is there. So, awed by the beauty and goodness of our children, dumbfounded by our failure to be the parents we hoped to be, worshipping, giving horsey rides, and picking up peas, we are brought to our knees.

—Polly Berrien Berends, *Gently Lead*

Prayer

Teach me the humility of a child, O God,
*   so that I may learn as the young do:*
With heart, mind, body, and soul,
*   and with complete willingness.*
Amen.

THE LORD PROVIDES

Isaiah 25:6

*On this mountain the Lord of hosts will make for
all peoples
a feast of rich food, a feast of well-aged
wines,
of rich food filled with marrow, of well-aged
wines strained clear.*

Our personal desert stories may relate vulnerabilities of spirit we call sin. We give in to the temptation of pride when we think we know what someone else needs, and more, when we see ourselves as the answer to that need. We fail to triumph over our personal evil or arrogance when we see ourselves as right or as having power over another. There are as many personal desert stories as there are persons. When they come to light, all we can say is, "Lord, have mercy."

Collectively, we have desert failures as well. When we think we have defeated an "enemy," when we have used violence in the name of righteousness, when we have succumbed to the temptation of dehumanizing those we have overpowered—as when we speak of "collateral damage" rather than human casualties or victims of war—when in our collective imagination we have become the Almighty, we have sinned and cry out, "Christ, have mercy."

Our personal and collective desert stories have another dimension too: the presence of a loving, forgiving God. God

provides us milk, honey, and manna in our desert and
nourishes us back to life. God is a lover of life who makes
the desert bloom, heals our wounded hearts, and restores our
faith in one another by encouraging us to look at others, as
ourselves. God is creator of the universe whose Spirit hovers
over creation. God is totally in love with creation and invites
us to be so, as well. It is God alone who can lead us out of
the desert, God alone who gives us new life and hope, God
alone who constantly beckons us so God does not have to do
this all alone!

—Martha Alken, *The Healing Power of Forgiving*

Prayer

The Lord is my shepherd, I shall not want.
*   He makes me lie down in green pastures;*
he leads me beside still waters;
*   he restores my soul.*
He leads me in right paths
*   for his name's sake.*

You prepare a table before me
*   in the presence of my enemies;*
you anoint my head with oil;
*   my cup overflows.*
Surely goodness and mercy shall follow me
*   all the days of my life,*
and I shall dwell in the house of the Lord
*   my whole life long.*

—Psalm 23:1-3, 5-6

PREACH BY EXAMPLE

Matthew 7:21, 24-25

*Not everyone who says to me, "Lord, Lord," will
enter the kingdom of heaven, but only the one
who does the will of my Father in heaven.*

*Everyone then who hears these words of
mine and acts on them will be like a wise man
who built his house on rock. The rain fell, the
floods came, and the winds blew and beat on
that house, but it did not fall, because it had
been founded on rock.*

We will make this year a year of peace, in a special way.
In order to be able to do that, we shall try to speak more to
God and with God, and less to and with human beings. Let
us preach the peace of Christ, as he did. He went about doing
good. He didn't give up his works of love just because the
Pharisees and others hated him or tried to ruin his Father's
work. He simply went around doing good.

Cardinal Newman has written: "Let me spread your
fragrance everywhere I go; let me preach, not with words,
but through example, through contagious strength, through
the invisible influence of what I do, through the visible
fullness of the love that my heart cherishes for you." Our
works of love are nothing but works of peace. Let us do
them with greater love and greater effectiveness, each and
every one of us in his or her daily work, in our home, with
our neighbor. It is always the same Christ who says:

24

I was hungry—not for food, but for the
peace that comes from a pure heart.
I was thirsty—not for water, but for the
peace that extinguishes the passionate thirst
for the passion of war.
I was naked—not stripped of clothing, but of
the beautiful dignity of men and women.
I was homeless—not without a roof made of
bricks, but without a heart that understands,
protects, and loves.

—Mother Teresa, *Mother Teresa: Love Stays*

Prayer

Come, you that are blessed by my Father,
inherit the kingdom prepared for you
from the foundation of the world;
for I was hungry and you gave me food,
I was thirsty and you gave me something to
drink,
I was a stranger and you welcomed me,
I was naked and you gave me clothing,
I was sick and you took care of me,
I was in prison and you visited me.

—Matthew 25:34-36

SEE WITH NEW EYES

Matthew 9:27-30

*As Jesus went on from there, two blind men
followed him, crying loudly, "Have mercy on us,
Son of David!" When he entered the house, the
blind men came to him; and Jesus said to them,
"Do you believe that I am able to do this?" They
said to him, "Yes, Lord." Then he touched their
eyes and said, "According to your faith let it be
done to you." And their eyes were opened.*

People of all faiths love St. Francis of Assisi because he
was a seer. For him every moment of life was an invitation to
intimacy with God, others, self, and the whole created world.
Routines that most saw as pointless and boring—like brick-
laying in a broken-down church—assumed for him a radiance beyond all telling.

Francis, like the spiritual masters of many traditions,
knew how important it was to develop the disposition of
concentrated awareness. Simply put, this means to see into
the ordinary as extraordinary. As we clear our "monkey
minds" of myriad distractions, as we learn to pay attention
and avoid dissipation, what we see may surprise us.

When we stop and think about it, we have to admit that
the mundane is a miracle. It puts us in touch with the "More
Than." There is an invisible depth, a wonder of being, a
mystery of dying and rising embedded in every created

person and action on Earth. We are all an immense intimate secret known only to God.

Most of the time we are not fully alive. We only exist. We are dazed by so much doing that we forget how to be. We lose our sense of gratitude for life's abundance. The air we breathe, the food we eat, the assistance available when we dial 911—all this and much more we take for granted.

We may even overlook the spectacular singularity of the people who love us. Before long we grow indifferent to the plight of the poor. We don't even thank waiters and waitresses for their service. It is as if we walk through life with opaque patches over our eyes.

There are so many ways to live intimately, why do we miss them? By this I mean to see into people, events, and things epiphanically. Poets and mystics catch in the familiar a glimpse, however fleeting, of the unfamiliar. Why don't we?

—Susan Muto, *Late Have I Loved Thee*

Prayer

Lord, Teach me to see
with a new set of eyes.
Make known your beauty to me
in all of creation;
And hide not your grace
that touches everything on earth
with the magnificence of your art.
Amen.

CIRCLE OF LIFE

Isaiah 30:23-24

*He will give rain for the seed with which you
sow the ground, and grain, the produce of the
ground, which will be rich and plenteous. On
that day your cattle will graze in broad pastures;
and the oxen and donkeys that till the ground
will eat silage, which has been winnowed with
shovel and fork.*

We as a people are only now beginning to learn to read
the language of the earth once again. We are beginning to see
what our actions create. Since the beginning there have been
those who have listened to earth's song. The cycles of our
life and the ceremony of honoring who we are as women, as
human beings, help us to become strong. We are a note in the
discord or in the harmony of this world. The way we walk is
the way it becomes. Speak in anger and anger will come to
you; speak with caring and love and these too shall be drawn
to you. Our choices in action are sacred. To choose to work
our way through our emotions and actions in a good way can
be a most sacred act. Each action affects all others. A single
drop of water reaches out to touch the very edge of the pool.

Look to the water, the sky, the earth! See them as a part
of your being, your life. Do not fear them; respect them. We
fool ourselves when we think we are learning to control the
earth. We must learn to use the language of the earth to

create a strong relationship. The flesh of Mother Earth becomes our flesh, the Spirit our spirit.

When I speak of these ways, I speak of power, the power of woman, not over another, but of gathering strength from within. I speak of the strength of the sacred hoop, of the home, the heart, and the land. Sharing the creative wealth and genius that lie within us all returns us to that sacred circle.

Our lives are circles, circles of the moon and the seasons, circles of family and community. We have worked side by side, sisters, mothers, neighbors, and friends, sharing joys and sorrows, works and talents. When the women are in harmony with the earth, we all are strong. We are within the circle of the heart, and a healing from within connects us. When the women are strong, they set the foundation of strength for the community. It was Grandmother Spider, in the Diné traditions, who wove the fabric of our world. We must weave harmony, not disharmony, into our lives. We must weave a wealth of beauty around us.

—Wendy Crockett, *Sweetwater Wisdom*

Prayer

*Teach me how to participate
    in the fullness of life, O God,
that I may share with my sisters and brothers
    all that has been given me.
Amen.*

ADVENT: A HOMECOMING

Mark 1:2-3

See, I am sending my messenger ahead of you,
who will prepare your way;
the voice of one crying out in the wilderness:
"Prepare the way of the Lord,
make his paths straight."

Something in us always needs to be called home. We need to see what or who we lack inside. Advent is a time to reclaim what we have lost in our hearts. It is not meant to be a cozy, self-satisfied time in which we wait for "Baby Jesus" to be born. The birth of Jesus is a historical event. Advent focuses instead on our own place of exile and whether or not this Savior who was born and lived on our earth has made a difference in our lives. Have we taken to heart the promises of hope that he held out to us? Do we have a great yearning in our heart for the sacred?

Advent is a season to remember that Jesus has already come and that he offered us many insights and examples for our own inner homecoming.

As we pray Advent, let us hold the consolations of God close to the exiled places of our hearts. God offers us light, consolation, and comfort for our homelessness. Advent is a time of homecoming, a time of joy and enthusiasm as we hear again God's promises to be with us and to resettle us in love.

As we watch the dance of snowflakes or the flicker of tree lights or the magic of a child's wondering eyes, let us see the deeper dance that is ever at play in our soul. The God of exiles calls us to dance our way home, to play upon the soil of our heart's sacred land. Emmanuel, God-with-us, shows us the way to the land of peace, to our true selves.

—Joyce Rupp, *May I Have This Dance?*

Prayer

God of exiles, keep calling us home.
You know the yearnings of our hearts.
You also know how easily we can lose our way.
May this Advent season be a time
of coming home to the best of who we are.
May our personal homecomings
influence all the earth.
We walk this day with hopeful hearts,
believing that your justice and compassion
will bring comfort and freedom
to all who are in exile.
Amen.

—Joyce Rupp, *May I Have This Dance?*

BE STRONG, FEAR NOT

Isaiah 35:3-4

Strengthen the weak hands,
and make firm the feeble knees.
Say to those who are of a fearful heart,
"Be strong, do not fear!
Here is your God.
He will come with vengeance,
with terrible recompense.
He will come and save you."

In the fifth century a female child was born to a family somewhere in the northeastern section of the Mediterranean world. They named her Elizabeth. She became a very learned young woman. When her parents died she gave away her possessions and entered a convent. Elizabeth was an ascetic, known for fasting, going barefoot, wearing the same garment repeatedly, and for her prayerfulness. Eventually she became abbess.

The emperor, Leo I, gave Elizabeth's convent a piece of land, ostensibly as an expression of respect for Elizabeth. But the land was inhabited by a large, fierce dragon. The dragon made the townspeople so afraid that they would not go out of the town.

Elizabeth went to the dragon's cave alone, carrying only a cross. She commanded the beast, "Come out!" After making the sign of the cross over the dragon, she grabbed it by the head, spit on it, and trampled it with her bare feet. Thus the new convent could be built and the townspeople could go out safely. Elizabeth became Elizabeth the Wonder-Worker.

Elizabeth is one of our foremothers, and we women of the Western Christian tradition in a time sixteen hundred years distant from hers need to claim her.

The story of Elizabeth suggests that she was in touch with power not available to the emperor or the men of the town. She slayed the dragon and was not afraid. Because of her the townspeople were freed to go out of the town and to make journeys. Elizabeth is in touch with a power that can deconstruct entire societies built on fear.

—Patricia O'Connell Killen, *Finding Our Voices*

Prayer

Those who love me, I will deliver;
I will protect those who know my name.
When they call to me, I will answer them;
I will be with them in trouble,
I will rescue them and honor them.
With long life I will satisfy them,
and show them my salvation.

—*Psalm 91:14-16*

RECOVER THE LOST

Matthew 18:12-14

If a shepherd has a hundred sheep, and one of them has gone astray, does he not leave the ninety-nine on the mountains and go in search of the one that went astray? And if he finds it, truly I tell you, he rejoices over it more than over the ninety-nine that never went astray. So it is not the will of your Father in heaven that one of these little ones should be lost.

What is it that keeps our hope alive and gets us through the tough things of midlife? I think that each of us has something or someone that gives us hope. This "reason for hoping" may be a person, or a special place, or a religious belief, or a vision of life that is strong enough to weather the internal storms and strife. There is an Ethiopian legend about a shepherd boy, Alemayu, that speaks to me of the power of hope. Alemayu had to spend the night on a bitterly cold mountain. He had only a very thin cloth to wear. To the amazement of all the villagers, he returned alive and well. When they asked him how he survived, he replied:

The night was bitter. When all the sky was dark, I thought I would die. Then far, far off I saw a shepherd's fire on another mountain. I kept my eyes on the red glow in the distance, and I dreamed of being warm. And that is how I had the strength to survive.

Each of us has a "shepherd's fire on another mountain" that has kept our hope alive. When the nights of our midlife have been dark and bitterly cold, we have seen something "far, far off" that has helped us survive. This "fire" has given us the courage to recover our lost self and to believe in the dreams that stir in our soul.

—Joyce Rupp, *Dear Heart, Come Home*

Prayer

Most loving God,
Grant me the courage
to recover what is lost,
what is hidden
in my heart.
Empower me to dream again,
to hope.
And allow me always
a reason to believe,
a purpose to live.
Amen.

A PLACE OF COMFORT

Matthew 11:28-30

*Come to me, all you that are weary and are
carrying heavy burdens, and I will give you rest.
Take my yoke upon you, and learn from me; for I
am gentle and humble in heart, and you will find
rest for your souls. For my yoke is easy, and my
burden is light.*

When friends of Christ come together for sharing,
laughter, discourse, and healthy debate, he is with us. An
aura of mutual respect for each one's dignity helps people
who were once strangers to be open and honest with one
another. By our words and our presence we show support for
each other's life call. Young and old, single or married,
female or male, we become a community of faith enjoying
the grace of spiritual friendship, for, in the words of Antoine
de Saint-Exupéry: "Love does not consist in gazing at each
other but in looking outward together in the same direction."

If we direct our eyes toward Jesus, we cannot be hurtful
to one another. In a spirit-filled atmosphere of mutual trust
and care, fraternal correction can be as healing as honest
conversation. There is no room in real relationships for
intimacy-deflating patterns of domination and submission.
The will to love others in the Lord precludes possessiveness
or crass put-downs.

The German poet Rilke wrote that in the state of friendship there is space and freedom for growth. Such a love, Rilke said, consists in this: "that two solitudes protect and touch and greet each other."

Being together in trustworthy intimacy teaches us to reappreciate the little things that make life great. How happy we are to speak from the heart and feel that we are really understood, to be ourselves without having to prove anything. The relaxation we need is enhanced by this atmosphere of mutual acceptance. We can let down our hair, as the expression goes, with no need to hide our vulnerability.

In the presence of friends who freely share their love for the Lord, we experience being drawn by grace into prayers of thanksgiving and genuine peace.

—Susan Muto, *Late Have I Loved Thee*

Prayer

Gracious Lord,
Lead me to a place
of comfort,
and of peace,
where respect and trust
for one another
are as bountiful
as your love for us.
Amen.

REVELATION

Isaiah 41:17-20

When the poor and needy seek water,
  and there is none,
    and their tongue is parched with thirst,
I the Lord will answer them,
  I the God of Israel will not forsake them.
I will open rivers on the bare heights,
  and fountains in the midst of the valleys;
I will make the wilderness a pool of water,
  and the dry land springs of water.
I will put in the wilderness the cedar,
  the acacia, the myrtle, and the olive;
I will set in the desert the cypress,
  the plane and the pine together,
so that all may see and know,
  all may consider and understand,
that the hand of the Lord has done this,
  the Holy One of Israel has created it.

Because the word of God is "alive and active" (Hebrews 4:12-13), it invites us to new discovery each time we encounter its power. We cannot predict where the Mystery will lead us. For every answer we receive, another question arises. No sooner is one need met than another presents itself.

God's silence is as intriguing as God's speaking. Silence ought not to be understood as a sign of rejection. Neither should it be for us a source of frustration. It is an invitation to return again to what it is that draws us inward. The full meaning of a religious experience may only be understood years after its initial occurrence.

For example, consider how long it took St. Augustine to understand his conversion experience in the garden or St. John of the Cross to grasp the meaning of his imprisonment in Toledo. New levels of meaning emerged for both saints because of their repeated dwelling on these watershed experiences.

The same is true in our own life. Every time we return to an epiphanic revelation, the door of insight opens a little more. Quiet rumination calms our concerns. We cease strenuous attempts to master the Mystery and start to appreciate the intricate tapestry woven by grace.

—Susan Muto, *Late Have I Loved Thee*

Prayer

Merciful God,
Help me to understand in my confusion,
And to trust in my questioning.
Be my peace in my frustration,
And my faith in my doubt.
Amen.

APPRENTICESHIP IN GOD

Isaiah 48:17

Thus says the Lord,
your Redeemer, the Holy One of Israel:
I am the Lord your God,
who teaches you for your own good,
who leads you in the way you should go.

The general vocation to follow Christ is lived in discipleship similar to an apprenticeship. In the Black Forest of Germany, a tourist can visit the many shops where carved wooden sculptures are sold. Today many items are machine made, but one can still find some handcrafted works, and these beautifully crafted items are prized for the skill of the sculptors who are able to carve delicate features into the wood. Tutoring under a master craftsman is required to master this art of wood carving. During the Middle Ages, a system of guilds existed to train aspiring young persons in the various crafts and trades. If a youth wanted to enter a certain profession, he was apprenticed to a master teacher. The stage of apprenticeship lasted from two to seven years and was followed by the journeyman stage. The apprentice would move into the home of the master teacher and learn the entire lifestyle of the craftsman, be he a wood-carver, carpenter, wood dyer, bookbinder, or weaver. Only after years of extensive and arduous training could one hope to become a master or craftsman. The guild system was a model of discipleship, of formation, and of education in that the apprentice was a disciple of the master.

Jesus calls Christians to follow him and to enter into a lifetime of discipleship. "Following" today is often considered a passive activity and is thought to show a lack of initiative. This is not the case in true discipleship because it is an active type of following. One follows in order to learn the skills of the master. If the disciple is attentive, he or she begins to think like the master, takes on the attitudes of the master, and eventually acquires the ways of the master. Such is the vocation to discipleship with Jesus. It is freely chosen by the disciple, but once entered, it must continually be rechosen—for the disciple always has more to learn. Like the apprentice, the disciple will need the discipline of hard work, attentiveness, and responsibility. Though the task is difficult, the disciple learns the mind and heart of Jesus through prayer, the scriptures, and liturgy. In time the disciple will experience a freedom of spirit. As the disciple embraces the Christian vocation, a fullness of humanity unfolds that brings peace, joy, and love.

—Elizabeth Willems, *Understanding Catholic Morality*

Prayer

Master Artist,
Direct me in the ways of your trade,
which is selflessness and perfect love,
and teach me the skills
of compassionate living.
Amen.

RECONCILIATION

Sirach 48:10

*At the appointed time, it is written, you are
destined
to calm the wrath of God before it breaks
out in fury,
to turn the hearts of parents to their children,
and to restore the tribes of Jacob.*

Healing family pain requires such intenseness as we look at the pain that has its source in a wounded root. Venturing through the roots of a family system calls for extreme patience, for we sit with an open wound. Clearing out the findings may bring to light family secrets that have greatly affected the way we deal with relationships, unconsciously causing isolation, alienation, anxiety, and division of loyalties among family members and across generations.

Bringing family secrets to light is not synonymous with indiscriminately hanging out the family's "dirty laundry." Everything need not be told to all, in the same way, for healing to happen. Honesty, discretion, and wisdom are crucial in confrontation. We do not seek to make amends directly when doing so would cause further injury to the person or others.

Families are the environment in which caring is expected, growth is smiled upon, and creativity either challenged or stifled. In the family, our primary community, forgiving becomes a means to new life and non-forgiving an occasion for building up resentment and anger, which lead to further negative consequences. Our negative feelings are complicated by the fact that each one of us also carries within us the unfinished business of previous generations.

I believe forgiving is healing for the soul. Forgiving is also healing for the system in that it alters negative patterns of behavior and demeaning relationships. The forgiving process in a family reminds me of the root canal. The system is changed from the inside out. The infection is cleared out, and the dentist can begin to rebuild the tooth structure. In forgiving, the body—the family—can again function according to its nature. And that is *good!*

Alla Bozath-Campbell writes, "Pain is always a symptom of some injury, an illness or a woundedness. . . . Paradoxically, the way past the pain is to go all the way through it." Forgiving and being forgiven alter our lives and effect healing among our loved ones.

—Martha Alken, *The Healing Power of Forgiving*

Prayer

Forgiving God,
Help me to love my family
with the same mercy
with which you love me.
Teach me in the ways of peace,
and healing,
and reconciliation.
Amen.

BE PATIENT, STAND FIRM

James 5:7-8

*Be patient, therefore, beloved, until the coming
of the Lord. The farmer waits for the precious
crop from the earth, being patient with it until it
receives the early and the late rains. You also
must be patient. Strengthen your hearts, for the
coming of the Lord is near.*

Commitment and enthusiasm are two concepts that are,
unfortunately, often confused. Commitment is that quality of
life that depends more on the ability to wait for something to
come to fulfillment—through good days and through bad—
than it does on being able to sustain an emotional extreme
for it over a long period of time. Enthusiasm is excitement
fed by satisfaction. The tangle of the two ideas, however, is
exactly what leads so many people to fall off in the middle
of a project.

When the work ceases to feel good, when praying for
peace gets nowhere, when the marriage counseling fails to
reinvigorate the marriage, when the projects and the plans
and the hopes worse than fail, they fizzle, that's when the
commitment really starts. When enthusiasm wanes and
romantic love dies and moral apathy—a debilitating loss of
purpose and energy—sets in, that is the point at which we
are asked to give as much as we get. That's when what we
thought was an adventure turns into a commitment. Some-

times a long, hard, demanding one that tempts us to despair. As if God will ever abandon the good. As if waiting for God's good time were a waste of our time. As if God's Word of love will ever fail us in the end.

Once upon a time, the dove said to the cloud, "How many snowflakes does it take to break a branch?" "I have no idea," the cloud replied. "I simply keep on snowing until it does." "Mmmmm," the little dove mused. "I wonder how many voices it will take before peace comes?"

Commitment is that quality of human nature that tells us not to count days or months or years, conversations or efforts or rejections but simply to go on going on until "all things are in the fullness of time," until everything is ready, until all hearts are in waiting for the Word of God in this situation to be fulfilled.

When we feel most discouraged, most fatigued, most alone is precisely the time we must not quit.

—Joan Chittister, *Songs of Joy*

Prayer

Teach me patience, O God,
and the discipline of commitment.
Encourage me to continue
in the hours and days of my frustration,
So that I may live to see
the fulfillment of my work,
the fruit of my labor.
Amen.

REMAIN TEACHABLE

Psalm 25:4-5, 8-9

Make me to know your ways, O Lord;
teach me your paths.
Lead me in your truth, and teach me,
for you are the God of my salvation;
for you I wait all day long.

Good and upright is the Lord;
therefore he instructs sinners in the way.
He leads the humble in what is right,
and teaches the humble his way.

When we first moved to Boulder, a Christian woman who later became a good friend offered me *The Autobiography of a Yogi*, a book written by the Hindu teacher Yogananda. Having just completed my graduate work in religious studies at Mundelein College, I told her, self-righteously, that I wasn't interested. With a smile she inquired, "Do you think it could be possible that God has something to teach you that you don't already know?" Wow! And then she continued, "I suggest you pray about it."

The song "The Rose" by Amanda Broom expresses best where my thinking was at that time. The song talks about a heart afraid of breaking, a dream afraid of waking, and a soul afraid of dying. Because of these fears, the song says that we never learn to dance; we are afraid to take a chance. "The Rose" describes exactly where I was in those days. I was afraid to step beyond the boundaries that I had accepted as a child in Sunday school. I had refused Christ's invitation to dance. I had not understood that Christianity is a living organism, not an organization, and that in order to keep pace with Spirit, old thought forms might have to die. I was afraid of waking.

Gradually it became clear to me that there were important concepts that I needed to examine beyond what I had learned. Slowly my fear left and I began to read the wonderful books, one by one, that my friend gave me. She lived high in the mountains and would lend me only one book at a time. She warned that, otherwise, I might get spiritual indigestion. It turned out to be a summer of timely awakening with lots of trips up the mountain.

—Betsy Serafin, *The Rose of Five Petals*

Prayer

Lord, It is I who am afraid
of waking from my dream,
of taking a chance,
of living to the full.
Extinguish my fear
so that I may learn to dance,
and to risk,
and to be fully alive.
Amen.

GOD IS WITH THE LOWLY

Zephaniah 3:11-13

I will remove from your midst
your proudly exultant ones,
and you shall no longer be haughty
in my holy mountain.
For I will leave in the midst of you
a people humble and lowly.
They shall seek refuge in the name of the Lord—
the remnant of Israel.

Reading the scriptures from the perspective of the poor makes it very clear that Jesus is on the side of the downtrodden and calls oppressors to conversion. A key text is the scene in Luke where, at the beginning of his ministry, Jesus goes to his home synagogue in Nazareth and reads from the scroll of Isaiah. Imagine how these words sound to people within a situation of oppression:

> The Spirit of the Lord is upon me, because he has anointed me to preach the good news to the poor; he has sent me to proclaim release to the captives and recovering of sight to the blind, to set at liberty those who are oppressed, to proclaim the acceptable year of the Lord.

Sitting down Jesus says, "Today this scripture is being fulfilled in your hearing" (Luke 4:16-21). This prophecy sets the agenda for Jesus' ministry, as we see from everything that follows in the gospels. His preaching that the reign of

God is near; his singling out the poor and those who hunger after justice for beatitude; the way he feeds and heals and welcomes outcasts—all of this reveals a choice, a preference for those who have not. Obviously, then, this is God's agenda for the poor: that they be released and set at liberty from grinding poverty and oppression. This is special good news for victims. It means that their present situation is not the last word about their lives, but that God has another design in mind. Touching structures as well as hearts, God is opening up a new future for the poor.

One of the most powerful expressions of this gospel truth is the Magnificat, the song of Mary. After praising God for all the great things He has done for her, a poor peasant woman, she goes on to sing about the great things God will do for everyone else, perceiving this in very startling words: "He has put down the mighty from their thrones and has exalted the lowly. He has filled the hungry with good things and has sent the rich away empty" (Luke 1:46-55). How does that sound to the hearts of those oppressed? There is a clear message enunciated here that rings all the way through the gospels: Jesus opts for the poor, for the cause of the poor, as the embodiment of God who does the same.

—Elizabeth A. Johnson, *Consider Jesus*

Prayer

Compassionate God,
You feed the hungry
with the Bread of Life,
and offer to the lowly
your Kingdom of Love.
Amen.

CREATOR GOD

Isaiah 45:6-7, 18

I am the Lord, and there is no other.
I form light and create darkness,
I make weal and create woe;
I the Lord do all these things.

For thus says the Lord,
who created the heavens
(he is God!),
who formed the earth and made it
(he established it;
he did not create it a chaos,
he formed it to be inhabited!):
I am the Lord, and there is no other.

Joining in the creative work is really central to the whole contemplative enterprise. Cosmogenesis—the generation of the cosmos—can be seen, as Teilhard de Chardin saw it, as "Christogenesis," the growth of the "ever greater Christ." This Christ has been "growing in stature and wisdom" (Luke 2:52; read "complexity and consciousness") these last dozen or so billion years and is nowhere near finished yet.

If I may modify Psalm 19 slightly, I will say: "The heavens declare the glory of God and the earth manifests the divine handiwork." What Earth and the other heavenly bodies are manifesting is the glory, the overflowing creative activity, that necessarily expresses and thus images the

Creator. If the Trinity-Creator so puts Its heart into the natural world, showing and revealing Itself on every side, displaying Its glory, then we certainly ought to pay attention, to learn as much as we can, and to appreciate the amazing variety, subtlety, niceness of adjustment and interrelation, beauty, capacity for development, novelty, inventiveness, and creativity in its turn of this cosmos.

It is, at the very least, the artwork of God, and if you know anything about art, you know how the artist is unavoidably present in the artwork, and how important it is to the artist that the artwork draw attention and succeed in communicating. Since the divine Artist has chosen to create, we cannot love the Artist without giving our best attention to the artwork.

—Beatrice Bruteau, *God's Ecstasy*

Prayer

Maker of this earth our home,
You sweep the heavens
with your starry skirt of night
and polish the eastern sky
to bring light to the new day.
Come to us in the birth
of the infant Christ:
that we discover the fullness
of your redemption
throughout the universe.

—Mary Kathleen Speegle Schmitt,
Seasons of the Feminine Divine

HOPE ABOUNDS

Isaiah 54:1

Sing, O barren one who did not bear;
burst into song and shout,
you who have not been in labor!
For the children of the desolate woman will be
more
than the children of her that is married, says
the Lord.

Hope is not just one single quality or promise. Hope has to do with believing beyond today—knowing there's a garden of beauty that awaits me. Hope encourages me to follow my dreams, to believe in the part of me that envisions my wholeness. Hope is trusting that what is happening will eventually make sense, or if it never does become meaningful, it will still offer an opportunity for growth. Hope assures me each morning that my life is of value no matter how unsettling or disturbing my current situation is. Hope encourages my heart not to give up and nudges me when it's time to move on. Hope doesn't need words or proofs or conditions. Hope accepts mystery and offers the gift of solid trust in the unknown. Hope doesn't pretend that I'll get all I want nor does hope deny that there will still be struggles down the road. Hope tucks promises of growth and truth inside the pockets of my struggles.

As I look back at my midlife journey, I realize I would never be who I am and where I am today if it had not been for hope. In the midst of many inner struggles, I had hope: of greater inner freedom when I felt strangled by my fears and weaknesses; of finding the truth of myself when I groped around in the cave of my darkness; of accepting my mortality when I encountered my own aging; of living my unspoken dreams even when I experienced failure and self-doubt; of living a more balanced life in the midst of my crazy busyness; of being at home with God as I shook off old ways of naming and relating to God; of being faithful to my significant relationships while I searched for the meaning of commitment and fidelity; of sharing my personal talents and gifts in a loving, generative way as I allowed myself to see my egocentricity.

Today I see that each of these dimensions of hope has become a reality in my life. Not that it's all accomplished and finished. Far from it. But I know that each of my hopes is greening and growing. . . . Many times I've found hope through things of the earth, or through something someone said to me, or through some passage that leapt at me from a page in a book. Sometimes it was just a whisper in my soul that promised me strength to get through the wilderness of my sadness and confusion.

—Joyce Rupp, *Dear Heart, Come Home*

Prayer

Father of Life,
Be my light
in the days of my darkness
And my hope
in the hours of my despair.
Amen.

MORAL LIVING

Isaiah 56:1-2

Thus says the Lord:
    Maintain justice, and do what is right,
for soon my salvation will come,
    and my deliverance be revealed.
Happy is the mortal who does this,
    the one who holds it fast,
who keeps the sabbath, not profaning it,
    and refrains from doing any evil.

Moral living is more than simply doing right actions as taught by our parents, teachers, and society. Some "right actions" may be "politically correct" or polite but lack the quality of moral life characterized by a disciple of Jesus Christ. We do not refrain from stealing because we do not want to get caught, be punished, and lose our reputation; rather, as Christians, we do not steal because we respect the property of others and love them as we love ourselves. We do not associate with members of a minority race because they serve our economic and social goals; rather we associate with all as colleagues, neighbors, and friends because each is equal and worthy in the eyes of the Lord. We do not downsize and lay off workers simply and primarily to keep a financial lead; rather, we strive to educate workers and keep them in the job market because it is just. We have responsibilities to workers because they are made in the image and likeness of God. Christian morality penetrates our mind and heart so that morally right actions emerge from personal conviction.

—Elizabeth Willems, *Understanding Catholic Morality*

Prayer

Walk in the way of the good,
*   and keep to the paths of the just.*
For the upright will abide in the land,
*   and the innocent will remain in it.*

Do not let loyalty and faithfulness forsake you;
*   bind them around your neck,*
*   write them on the tablet of your heart.*
So you will find favor and good repute
*   in the sight of God and of people.*
Trust in the Lord with all your heart,
*   and do not rely on your own insight.*
In all your ways acknowledge him,
*   and he will make straight your paths.*

—Proverbs 2:20-21, 3:3-6

LET IT BE

Luke 1:38

Here am I, the servant of the Lord; let it be with me according to your word.

It is done, irreversible, time altered, incarnation. God is made flesh and dwells among us. God is human and hiding in the world in a woman of Nazareth, a town in the middle of nowhere, among a people oppressed and burdened and of little or no worth, chosen and favored to bring light into the world and shatter the darkness. Mary surrenders, obeys—she has listened, heard, and taken the words to heart, so single-mindedly that the Word becomes flesh in her. In a moment it is done. She is mother, maidservant, prophet, bearer of hope to her people, a light to the nations—and in danger.

In the Gospel of Luke, the annunciation is the only time Mary sees or hears the angel or has the vision. From now on she lives with the Word, surrendering in obedience to an ever growing and maturing understanding of the Word in her life and in the world. The seed is planted, and it will bear fruit in her child and in her life as disciple and believer.

Mary gives her word and keeps it. Her life is no longer defined by being a virgin engaged to Joseph. She is a servant of the living God, a prophet of the Most High, the bearer of the seed of justice and judgment and the hope of the nations.

Her new life, her new relationship to God, has begun. She lives now on the word and obeys, doing for God and her people what they have believed in and hoped for ages.

"Let it be done to me as you have said." This is Mary's acknowledgment of belief, her baptism, her confession of faith, her proclamation of hope in God. They are the words of the Christian community in her mouth: a post-resurrection statement of Christ, the Lord, the Son of God. She is the first person to hear the gospel and take it to heart. She believes in what God will do, in her child to come. She believes it changes everything, including first of all who she is and what she is to be. She is the highly favored daughter of God, full of grace. Each of us shares that moment of belief with Mary at our baptism, when we too become the children of God, full of grace and freedom, by the power of the Spirit that overshadows us and comes to dwell with us.

—Megan McKenna, *Mary: Shadow of Grace*

Prayer

Mary, Mother of God,
Grant me the courage to say yes to God
as you did,
and to live according to the Word.
Let me utter with you the holy words
you spoke to the angel Gabriel:
"Let it be done,"
the words that forever changed history
and brought forth to our world
the Savior and Redeemer of Life.
Amen.

DEFEND THE AFFLICTED

Psalm 72:3-4

*May the mountains yield prosperity for the
    people,
    and the hills, in righteousness.
May he defend the cause of the poor of the
    people,
    give deliverance to the needy,
    and crush the oppressor.*

"Who do you say that I am?" In Latin American libera-
tion theology the question begins to be answered by bringing
into focus the poverty of millions of people. The question
arises: is it God's will that these people be deprived of
livelihood, that they be malnourished, that children die, that
there be inadequate education, no medical benefits, no
shelter for millions of people? Is this what God desires? No,
it is wrong. Then why is it like this? At this point social
analysis starts to uncover economic and political structures
wherein the majority of people are landless while a small
minority of people own all the land. The land itself is
worked by the many for the benefit of the few. This in itself
is a controversial analysis. The dispute over its legitimacy
brings to mind Brazilian Bishop Dom Helder Camara's
comment: "When I ask people for bread to feed the poor,
they think I am a saint; when I ask them *why* the poor are
hungry, they think I am a Communist." But it is that asking

of the question *why* that gets to the root causes. Then it becomes possible to envision something besides just emergency measures and endless patching up; a radical, creative quest for better structures ensues.

—Elizabeth A. Johnson, *Consider Jesus*

Prayer

Liberator of the Dispossessed,
You look with pity on the victims
    of this world,
and restore them to the fortune
    of original blessing.
Make your steadfast love to well up in us:
that, ministering to those who are afflicted,
we come to know You as our deepest truth.

—Mary Kathleen Speegle Schmitt,
Seasons of the Feminine Divine

EMMANUEL: GOD WITH US

Matthew 1:23

"Look, the virgin shall conceive and bear
a son,
and they shall name him Emmanuel,"
which means, "God is with us."

Knowing what it means to bring forth life we will be unwilling to destroy life. There is a strong urge in us to tell our story. Doing so we would be reclaiming a very old wisdom. Stories about birth, which are now exceptional and marginal, made up a large part of the stories which formed us. The Hebrew scriptures are full of stories about the births of babies. In such a tradition of celebrating birth it would not have occurred to people to imagine that they were self-sufficient. They recognized the breath of life as God's gift and celebrated the fragile vulnerable wonder of new life.

Contemporary culture regards births and babies as the business of mothers but Israel's wisdom suggests that births belong to the creative process of God. Biblical theologian Phyllis Trible draws the implications even further when she shows that the Hebrew plural for the word *womb* is the same as the word for *compassion*. This organ which is unique to the female becomes a metaphor to express the compassion and the love of God. The God in whom we live and move and have our being is a God of womb-like love—a God who will hold us close, and who, in love, will withdraw, will contract her womb and give birth to us.

—Anne Thurston, *Because of Her Testimony*

Prayer

God-with-us
is the Word-made-flesh,
steadfast love,
mother-love,
love incarnate,
the love one has
for a child in the womb,
on whom we depend
like a child in the womb,
in whom we live
and move
and have our being,
the Holy
and wholly Other.

—Miriam Therese Winter,
WomanPrayer, WomanSong

FERTILITY

Judges 13:2-3, 24

There was a certain man of Zorah, of the tribe of the Danites, whose name was Manoah. His wife was barren, having borne no children. And the angel of the Lord appeared to the woman and said to her, "Although you are barren, having borne no children, you shall conceive and bear a son."

The woman bore a son, and named him Samson. The boy grew, and the Lord blessed him.

My experience in this life is in the body of mother, lover, sister, and wife. This life has taught me much about emotions and behavior in our human tribe. Carrying the life of the people has been a blessing I'll always be grateful for. Women have carried the future of life in our wombs from the beginning of time.

A woman carries *Tah m'ne*, womb, a strong, fibrous basket of water that nurtures life. This openness within us is what makes us strong in our creative, nurturing, and intuitive nature. When we see the moon pass through the phases of light and shadow, our bodies respond. Our bodies, both male and female, change chemically, mentally, and physically. The water in our bodies is affected much like the oceans, drawn toward surrounding planets. Tides rise highest during the full moon. Water is the element most often related to emotion. Our emotions swell and recede as we struggle to survive the tests of our lives and the cycles of the moon.

Women embody the circle of life. Their moon cycle creates potential life in the egg and, with the moonflow, a doorway between worlds. At this doorway the energies mingle, the physical and spiritual life and what we know as death. When used in a respectful way, this circle can open us to the spiritual direction and vision we seek.

—Wendy Crockett, *Sweetwater Wisdom*

Prayer

Womb of All,
in the midst of a failing world
You draw us into community with You
*   and one another.*
Contain us with the faithfulness
*   of your motherly-compassion:*
that, nurtured by your care,
*   we mother all who are in need*
*   of groundedness in You.*

—Mary Kathleen Speegle Schmitt,
Seasons of the Feminine Divine

MOTHERHOOD

Luke 1:31-32, 36-37

*You will conceive in your womb and bear a son,
and you will name him Jesus. He will be great,
and will be called the Son of the Most High, and
the Lord God will give to him the throne of his
ancestor David. . . . And now, your relative
Elizabeth in her old age has also conceived a
son; and this is the sixth month for her who was
said to be barren. For nothing will be impossible
with God.*

The spiritual journey of motherhood looks beyond the
interpersonal story of a mother and a baby to see the univer-
sal truths underlying and manifesting through the human
experiences. Being a mother is thus lifted off the nuts-and-
bolts level of the management of children to a level of
transcendental discovery that incidentally blesses and
enhances the human experience at every point. None of us
starts out knowing how to be a mother. The experience
makes the mother by allowing her to discover her qualities
and capacities from that particular standpoint. Likewise, no
one starts out understanding what it means that "God is
Love." But if we go into motherhood seeing it as a process
of spiritual growth and discovery, we will find each stage
teaching us more about Love as a reality that is present even
when we personally can't seem to come up with it. We will
discover that it is this divine Love and Intelligence that

raises our children. And, in that discovery, we will find ourselves divinely nurtured and matured as well.

The marvelous expansion of awareness called being a mother feels like a crisis to our human sense of ourselves at every point where that old sense is challenged by the new unfoldment. It is the nature of human ego sense to resist change because it alters our picture of who and what we are. And we like to be certain of who we are, even if the picture isn't altogether positive. By definition then, ego sense strives to keep its view of things constant, and this means limited. It feels comfortable only with the known, and what doesn't fit its picture will make it feel uncomfortable. Yet expansion is the nature of Life, because Life lives to bloom. Seeing more and more of what really is—despite the human, limited beliefs—is what makes our human experiences fruitful and fulfilled. We bloom by seeing.

—Ann Tremaine Linthorst,
Mothering As a Spiritual Journey

Prayer

Mother of the Universe,
even before we were conceived
You knew us by name
as your daughters and sons.
Cradle us in your goodness
and love:
that, binding creation to yourself,
all humanity discover the joy
of wholeness in You.

—Mary Kathleen Speegle Schmitt,
Seasons of the Feminine Divine

SEE THE BEAUTY

Song of Songs 2:10-14

My beloved speaks and says to me:
"Arise, my love, my fair one,
*   and come away;*
for now the winter is past,
*   the rain is over and gone.*
The flowers appear on the earth;
*   the time of singing has come,*
and the voice of the turtledove
*   is heard in our land.*
The fig tree puts forth its figs,
*   and the vines are in blossom;*
*   they give forth fragrance.*
Arise, my love, my fair one,
*   and come away.*
O my dove, in the clefts of the rock,
*   in the covert of the cliff,*
let me see your face,
*   let me hear your voice;*
for your voice is sweet,
*   and your face is lovely."*

"Look at that bush!" I said to my husband as we walked
to the beach one day. The bush was a mass of flame-red
flowers. Framed by the cloudless blue sky, the hibiscus had
filled me with awe and wonder. And it reminded me of the
verse . . . "See how the lilies of the field grow . . . not even
Solomon in all his splendor was dressed like one of these"
(Matthew 6:28-29).

Later, I watched a small boy paddle in the sea, fill his bucket with water and shingle and, with a smile of pure delight stretching from one ear to the other, bring these treasures back to his elderly grandmother. As he fingered the water and contemplated the multicolored stones he had captured, her wrinkled face lit up too. These two were relishing "the now," attentive to what they could see and feel. Jesus' invitation to learn the ABC of prayer by looking at the lilies or by looking at the birds encourages us to do the same. Looking not only prepares us for stillness, it is important in itself.

Some people call this mindfulness. As Brother Ramon puts it in *Heaven on Earth*, mindfulness means "to enter into, to enjoy, to absorb what is immediately before you. . . ." He adds that to chop an onion, peel a turnip, grate a carrot, and scrub a potato, if done in mindfulness, "can be an act of meditation and a source of tranquillity and thankfulness."

The secret of this kind of prayer is to be alert to our surroundings as that little boy on the beach, to drink in the beauty before us, to pay attention to the sounds we so often ignore and to make it possible for all our senses to become aids to prayer: touch, smell, imagination, and emotions.

—Joyce Huggett, *Learning the Language of Prayer*

Prayer

How beautiful you are, my love,
how very beautiful!

—*Song of Songs 4:1*

THE SONG OF MARY

Luke 1:46-49

My soul magnifies the Lord,
and my spirit rejoices in God my Savior,
for he has looked with favor on the lowliness of
his servant.
Surely, from now on all generations will call
me blessed;
for the Mighty One has done great things for me,
and holy is his name.

Mary sings, but she does not sing only for herself. She sings for her people. She preaches in song and joy. She prophetically announces what is to come, what will take place in the future, and what is already beginning in her flesh and blood. She speaks of her child and the three turnings, the three revolutions that he will set in motion in the world: the turning of the heart, the turning of politics and power, and the turning of hunger and economics.

In Elizabeth's presence Mary can sing, borrowing from the ancient traditions of Israel, the battle song of Hannah (from Samuel) and about what God does in history using simple folk who believe and hope. She is careful to begin: "My soul proclaims the greatness of the Lord, my spirit exults in God my savior! He has looked upon his servant in her lowliness and people forever will call me blessed. The Mighty One has done great things for me, Holy is his Name!

From age to age his mercy extends to those who live in his presence." She is great because God has taken notice of her. God thinks of her! She is not great because of anything she does or will do, but because God includes her in the marvelous work of salvation and wonders. And so she proclaims aloud the great works of God and what has been done for her, in her, and what God will do in her child for the rest of the world. She is prophet, and she comes right to the point: God has acted with power and done wonders, scattering the proud with their plans.

The song of Mary also expresses the deepest feeling of the Christian soul. There is a time for us to seek truth, to discover what our major duties are, and to become truly and essentially human. There is a time for asking from and serving God. We come to understand that divine love seeks out that which is poorer and weaker in order to fill it and make it great.

—Megan McKenna, *Mary: Shadow of Grace*

Prayer

Hail Mary, full of grace,
the Lord is with thee;
blessed art thou among women
and blessed is the fruit
of thy womb, Jesus.
Holy Mary, Mother of God,
pray for us sinners,
now and at the hour of our death.
Amen.

PURIFICATION

Malachi 3:2-4

*He is like a refiner's fire and like fullers' soap:
he will sit as a refiner and purifier of silver, and
he will purify the descendants of Levi and refine
them like gold and silver, until they present
offerings to the Lord in righteousness. Then the
offering of Judah and Jerusalem will be pleasing
to the Lord as in the days of old.*

Jesus not only said, "When you pray . . ." Almost in the same breath, he continues, "When you fast . . ." He did not say, "If you fast . . ." but, "When you fast . . ." It was as though, in his mind, fasting and prayer are two sides of the same coin. Furthermore, when John's disciples asked why his disciples did not fast, Jesus replied: "How can the guests of the bridegroom mourn while he is with them? The time will come when the bridegroom will be taken from them; then they will fast."

One reason why fasting is valuable is that it helps to expose the things that control us. Food so easily camouflages and quietens emotions which consume us: anger, impatience, anxiety, loneliness, self-loathing. If we decide to deprive the body of one meal a week or of all meals one day a week, these obsessional feelings will rise to the surface. Although this can be distressing, it reveals some of the hindrances to our prayer life we need to deal with. But fasting has a positive face too. It sharpens our concentration so that we can use the time we would have spent preparing or eating food praising God and deepening our relationship with him.

—Joyce Huggett, *Learning the Language of Prayer*

Prayer

Yet even now, says the Lord,
    return to me with all your heart,
with fasting, with weeping, and with mourning;
    rend your hearts and not your clothing.
Return to the Lord, your God,
    for he is gracious and merciful,
slow to anger, and abounding in steadfast love,
    and relents from punishing.

—Joel 2:12-13

ACTS OF KINDNESS

Luke 1:68, 78-79

Blessed be the Lord God of Israel,
for he has looked favorably on his people
and redeemed them.

By the tender mercy of our God,
the dawn from on high will break upon us,
to give light to those who sit in darkness and in
the shadow of death,
to guide our feet into the way of peace.

In Melbourne I visited an old man, who nobody knew existed. I saw that his room was in wretched shape, and I wanted to clean it up. He stopped me: "I'm doing fine." I didn't say anything, and finally he let me do it. In his room there was a wonderfully beautiful lamp, all covered with dust. I asked him: "Why don't you turn this lamp on?" "For whom? Nobody ever visits me." Then I asked him: "Will you light the lamp if the sisters come to visit you?" "Yes, if I hear a human voice, I'll turn it on." Recently he sent word to me: "Tell my friend that the lamp she turned on in my life is still burning."

These are the people whom we have to get to know. If we do get to know them, we'll learn to love them, and this love will teach us to serve them. Let's not be satisfied with just giving them money. Money isn't enough. You can always earn money. But they need your hands, so that you can serve them. They need your hearts, so that you can love them.

—Mother Teresa, *Mother Teresa: Love Stays*

Prayer

Dear Lord, may I see you today and every day in the person of your sick and, as I nurse them, may I serve you. Even when you present yourself in the unhandsome disguise of the irritable, the demanding, or the unreasonable, may I recognize you and say: "Jesus, my patient one, how sweet it is to serve you."

Lord, give me this seeing faith; then my work will never get tedious. I will always find joy in bearing the moods and fulfilling the wishes of all poor sufferers.

O dear sick people, how doubly dear you are to me, when you embody Christ; and what an advantage it is for me to be allowed to care for you.

Lord, make me receptive to the dignity of my high calling and to its many responsibilities. Don't allow me to dishonor them by slipping into coldness, unfriendliness, and impatience.

And, O God, since you, Jesus, are my patient one, deign to be a patient Jesus to me as well. Be indulgent with my mistakes, and look to my intention of loving you and of serving you in the person of each one of your sick.

Lord, increase my faith, bless my efforts and my work, now and forever. Amen.

—Mother Teresa, *Mother Teresa: Love Stays*

A SAVIOR IS BORN

Luke 2:10-11

I am bringing you good news of great joy for all the people: to you is born this day in the city of David a Savior, who is the Messiah, the Lord.

The story of Christmas is the story that God has been trying to tell us since the very beginning of time. On the last Sunday before Christmas Day the church tries to help us remember and tells us to start believing the stories again. The angel Gabriel tells Mary "nothing is impossible with God," so in the week before the birth of God in the world in a human child we have to practice believing that nothing is impossible.

At Christmas we celebrate. We celebrate the fact that Mary said yes. We can almost imagine Mary looking at the angel Gabriel and saying, "Tell God I say yes." But we also celebrate the fact that every one of us said yes in our baptism. We said yes, we believe the story of incarnation, of God becoming human and dwelling among us, and we believe in hope and peace with justice here on earth for all. We tell God we'll obey; we've listened and we say yes. Like Mary, we say: "We are the servants of the Lord. Let it be done unto us according to your word." It makes an incredible difference in history that Mary said yes. It makes an incredible difference in this world that we say yes, today, and make the story keep coming true in our lives.

What if we, who are nothing alone, are the difference between the way the world is now and the coming of peace on earth? What if we are the difference between darkness pervading the world or light coming into the world? At Christmas we celebrate the fact that Mary said yes. Will we tell God that we too say yes? If we do, perhaps the story will come true in ways none of us ever thought about, and the world will know that nothing is impossible with God—and that God needs us to make all the stories come true.

—Megan McKenna, *Mary: Shadow of Grace*

Prayer

A child has been born for us,
a son given to us;
authority rests upon his shoulders;
and he is named
Wonderful Counselor, Mighty God,
Everlasting Father, Prince of Peace.

—Isaiah 9:6

BE A PROPHET

Matthew 10:18-20

*You will be dragged before governors and kings
because of me, as a testimony to them and the
Gentiles. When they hand you over, do not worry
about how you are to speak or what you are to
say; for what you are to say will be given to you
at that time; for it is not you who speak, but the
Spirit of your Father speaking through you.*

The Oxford Companion to the Bible suggests that the
emotional power of Jeremiah 20, and several other chapters
in the book that evoke the tensions of a prophet's calling,
comes from the fact that "behind the apparently untroubled
certainty of 'Thus says the Lord,' there may lie a host of
unresolved questions and deep inner turmoil."

In our own time we look for peace and healing, but our
newspapers are filled with tales of violence and rage. And
Jeremiah holds this world up to us, as a mirror. Hearing his
words every morning . . . I also recognized . . . the public
dimension of his prophecy and of our response. Jeremiah's
lament over a land so ravaged that even the birds and ani-
mals have fled has a powerful resonance in an age in which
species are rapidly disappearing, and the threat of nuclear
warfare remains. His bleak image of death "cutting down the
children in the street, young people in the squares, the
corpses of the slain like dung on a field, like sheaves behind

the harvester, with no one to harvest them" (9:21-22) could have come from a *Newsweek* story on Bosnia, or Rwanda, or inner-city America.

The contemporaneity of Jeremiah made me reflect on our need for prophets; I'd sit in the monks' choir and let the naive thoughts come: *it really is this bad, and if people heard it they would want to change; they'd have to change.* Of course it was Jeremiah himself who'd bring me back to earth, to the bitterness of his call, when God tells him: "You shall speak to them and they will not listen; you shall call and they shall not answer" (7:27). Yet a prophet speaks out of hope and, like all the prophets, Jeremiah's ultimate hope is for justice, a people made holy by "doing what is right and just in the land" (33:15). As the carriers of hope through disastrous times, prophets are a necessary other. And we reject them because they make us look at the way things really are; they don't allow us to deny our pain.

—Kathleen Norris, *The Cloister Walk*

Prayer

O Lord, you have enticed me,
*   and I was enticed;*
you have overpowered me,
*   and you have prevailed.*
I have become a laughingstock all day long;
*   everyone mocks me.*
For whenever I speak, I must cry out,
*   I must shout, "Violence and destruction!"*
For the word of the Lord has become for me
*   a reproach and derision all day long.*

—Jeremiah 20:7-8

FELLOWSHIP IN GOD

1 John 1:1-3

*We declare to you what was from the beginning,
what we have heard, what we have seen with our
eyes, what we have looked at and touched with
our hands, concerning the word of life—this life
was revealed, and we have seen it and testify to
it, and declare to you the eternal life that was
with the Father and was revealed to us—we
declare to you what we have seen and heard so
that you also may have fellowship with us; and
truly our fellowship is with the Father and with
his Son Jesus Christ.*

The journey toward wise faith changes a woman. Beginning this journey means entering a process of ongoing transformation in which her relationship to herself and her religious heritage is recast. As a woman progresses along this journey she may find herself gradually becoming capable of both criticism and creativity, more honest about reality, and more hopeful about possibilities that can arise even from death.

To take this path we will need to attend more closely to our own experiences of God, to our relationships to our Christian tradition, and to the experiences of our foremothers in faith. In community with them and with our sisters in faith today we will find support and resist self-deception as we move through our experience of simultaneous desire and disillusionment. In community with them we begin to discover that ambiguity has always been the context within which women have journeyed toward God. When we attend to their journeys we may discover important things about our foremothers; their lives contained much more than we have been told or been willing to see.

We must turn to our mothers and foremothers and see their humanity and their faith in its own terms. They are our forbearers. They are our companions. Their stories provide us an alternative context for exploring and defining our reality. . . . Dimensions of our mothers' stories show us things we did not know about our own. Reflection on our own experiences allows us to notice things not seen in their stories. Understanding and giving voice to our own and our mothers' experiences as women of faith . . . is the process that can lead toward wisdom.

—Patricia O'Connell Killen, *Finding Our Voices*

Prayer

For just as the body is one and has many
members, and all the members of the body,
though many, are one body, so it is with Christ.
For in the one Spirit we were all baptized into
one body—Jews or Greeks, slaves or free—and
we were all made to drink of one Spirit.
Indeed, the body does not consist of one
member but of many.

—*1 Corinthians 12:12-14*

GOD IS LIGHT

1 John 1:5

*This is the message we have heard from him and
proclaim to you, that God is light and in him
there is no darkness at all.*

Before there was sun, moon, or stars, God began creation with an outburst of Being, declaring, "Let there be
light," and there was light. Then the light was separated from
the darkness, setting the scene for what was to come. In
omniscience, God knew and awaited the Fall, humanity's
apparent separation from God.

We no longer remember who we are. We have forgotten
that we can enjoy a divine relationship with God. We have
forgotten we are Spirit and that we can walk on water. We
have joined forces with the world and learned how mediocre
the life of the flesh can be. We live in loneliness, deception,
and illusion. From the time of the Fall until the coming of
Jesus . . . we have immersed ourselves in darkness and in
what appears to be separation from God and from one
another.

Mystical Judaism, when speaking in dualistic terms,
believes that it is we who create benevolent and malevolent
entities with our thoughts, which then support our actions in

either a negative or a positive way. . . . And if it is true that we have created benevolent and malevolent entities with our thoughts, then we can exorcise them with our thoughts. All, even the illusion, is for our spiritual growth.

But I do pray daily for protection, even from the illusion, which seems so real. I cast out any spirit of darkness that might have entered during the night. And then I surround myself with the light of Christ for protection throughout the day. When we walk in Christ's light, darkness cannot touch us, for darkness cannot enter an arena of pure Light.

—Betsy Serafin, *The Rose of Five Petals*

Prayer

Dawn of Glory,
You call us from the Shadow
of your wings of night
to sing and dance to the melodies
of your love and faithfulness.
Save us from the times of trouble:
that, absorbing the wisdom
of your compassion,
we rise above all that would confuse
and destroy us,
and enter into the radiance
of the Land of your Shalom.

—Mary Kathleen Speegle Schmitt,
Seasons of the Feminine Divine

DISCIPLESHIP

1 John 2:3-6

Now by this we may be sure that we know [Jesus Christ], if we obey his commandments. Whoever says, "I have come to know him," but does not obey his commandments, is a liar, and in such a person the truth does not exist; but whoever obeys his word, truly in this person the love of God has reached perfection. By this we may be sure that we are in him: whoever says, "I abide in him," ought to walk just as he walked.

Discipleship means taking on a new way of life that encompasses all of one's moral sensibilities. As one learns the mind of Jesus one begins to evaluate moral dilemmas with the mind and heart of Jesus. One begins to love and care and become responsible for people in the manner of Jesus. When these actions are done in faith, they reflect the moral stand of Jesus. The Christian disciple can give money to the United Way because everyone at the office is donating, but that same disciple can also give because he or she wants to help brothers and sisters in need. It is evident, then, that Christian discipleship encompasses more than performing moral actions. . . .

The apprenticeship for a Christian disciple does not end with Christian education but is a lifelong enterprise of seeing in each new situation the concrete calling to respond with time, energy, material help, and spiritual support. H. Richard Niebuhr in his classic text, *The Responsible Self*, articulates this well in saying, "God is acting in all actions upon you. So respond to all actions upon you as to respond to his action." Christian vocation is basically *a call to love and to put on the mind and heart of Jesus*.

—Elizabeth Willems, *Understanding Catholic Morality*

Prayer

Holy Master,
Direct me toward true discipleship,
so that I may learn
right living
and just actions.
Teach me according to the Word
so that by my faith
I may be an example
of your love.
Amen.

PURSUE THE THINGS OF GOD

1 John 2:15-17

*Do not love the world or the things in the world.
The love of the Father is not in those who love
the world; for all that is in the world—the desire
of the flesh, the desire of the eyes, the pride in
riches—comes not from the Father but from the
world. And the world and its desire are passing
away, but those who do the will of God live
forever.*

We live in a culture that conspires against us. Every day
advertising agencies tell us that we need just one more thing
to be truly happy. We need to do one more thing, they advise
us, if we want to be really successful. We need to achieve
one more thing in our lives, they insist, if we are to be totally
valuable people. Hardly anyone ever tells us that we're fine
just the way we are—thin or hefty, introverted or extro-
verted, shy or sociable. So we spend our lives trying to
reshape ourselves or, barring that, trying to hide the shape
we're in from the gaze of those who know from the same ads
what it is we're lacking.

It's the awareness of inadequacy that leaves us feeling
disadvantaged. It's the absence of satisfaction with ourselves
that drives us to measure ourselves by those around us—and
find ourselves deficient.

The ancients called the failure to pursue the things of God or to recognize the obstacles to union with God in our own lives "spiritual blindness." And that it surely is. But it is just as surely true that failing to recognize the stuff of union with God that lies within us is spiritual blindness as well.

Psalm 16 calls us to be what we are with full confidence that it is precisely in the configuration of qualities that we call "ourselves" that we will find the God who is leading us to their fullness. Running away from ourselves, no matter how well intentioned, becomes instead a flight from the spiritual life. Then, after we have worked so hard to be richer, thinner, faster, and louder, we wonder how it is that we can have everything—and still feel empty.

—Joan Chittister, *Songs of Joy*

Prayer

The Lord is my chosen portion and my cup;
*   you hold my lot.*

I bless the Lord who gives me counsel;
*   in the night also my heart instructs me.*
I keep the Lord always before me;
*   because he is at my right hand,*
*   I shall not be moved.*
Therefore my heart is glad, and my soul rejoices;
*   my body also rests secure.*

You show me the path of life.
*   In your presence there is fullness of joy;*
in your right hand are pleasures forevermore.

—Psalm 16:5, 7-9, 11

GOD IS PRESENT IN ALL

John 1:1-5

*In the beginning was the Word, and the Word
was with God, and the Word was God. He was in
the beginning with God. All things came into
being through him, and without him not one
thing came into being. What has come into being
in him was life, and the life was the light of all
people. The light shines in the darkness, and the
darkness did not overcome it.*

We dream of times gone by when there used to be a
palpable sense of belonging to some great wholeness that
was meaningful in itself and extended its meaningfulness to
us. Keiji Nishitani describes it as a feeling that all of us, not
just human beings, but all living things, were living from the
same life, like leaves on a single tree. Each soul was life
itself, taking some particular form, whether human, animal,
or plant. This was the basis for a "sympathetic affinity"
among the living, indicating a unity deeper than our every-
day superficial relations. The mysterious wholeness, beyond
our individual selves, was the sacred, and we felt it as such.
Can we not have that anymore?

Somewhere deep down, we are all filled with mystical
longing, longing for meaningful belonging, for profound
union, longing to be securely embedded in the ultimate
meaningfulness, and therefore we need to see all our world

in that context. We long to feel the ultimate meaningfulness as real, all around us, concrete, real, intimate, tangible, communicating with us. To attain this in today's climate, we need a new theology of the cosmos, one that is grounded in the best science of our day. It will be a theology in which God is very present, precisely in all the dynamisms and patterns of the created order, in which God is not rendered absent by the self-organizing activities of the natural world, but in which God is actual as the one who makes and the one who is incarnate in what is made by these very self-making activities.

—Beatrice Bruteau, *God's Ecstasy*

Prayer

In the beginning,
before the birdsong
or the breath of life
lifted its gift
to the warmth of the sun:
In the beginning
was the Word
and the Word was with God
when God established the heavens,
when God drew a circle on the face of the deep,
when God marked out the foundations of
    the earth,
the Word was with God,
and the Word was God.

—Miriam Therese Winter,
WomanPrayer, WomanSong

A MOTHER'S PAIN

Luke 2:33-35

The child's father and mother were amazed at what was being said about [Jesus]. Then Simeon blessed them and said to his mother Mary, "This child is destined for the falling and the rising of many in Israel, and to be a sign that will be opposed so that the inner thoughts of many will be revealed—and a sword will pierce your own soul too."

Thanks to the shape and creative potential of their own bodies, women know the pain of bringing new life into the world. . . . In a way unique to half the human race, women labor in bearing and birthing each new generation, a suffering which can be woven round with a strong sense of creative power and joy.

When actively engaged and experienced, however, this experience of labor and delivery offers a superb metaphor for Sophia-God's struggle to birth a new people, even a new heaven and a new earth. One biblical text makes this explicit as God says: "For a long time I have held my peace, I have kept still and restrained myself; now I will cry out like a woman in labor, I will gasp and pant" (Isaiah 42:14).

The loud birthing cries evoke a God who is in hard labor, sweating, pushing with all her might to bring forth justice, the fruit of her love. Intense suffering as an ingredient in intense creative power marks the depth of divine involvement in the process. And it is not over yet; only eschatologically will the delivery take place. In the course of history human beings are partners with Holy Wisdom in the birthing process, sharing in the labor of liberating life for a new future.

—Elizabeth A. Johnson, *She Who Is*

Prayer

Jesus fixed his eyes on his disciples, and said:
"Blessed are you that weep now,
for one day you will laugh.
Woe to you that laugh now,
for you will mourn and weep."
"Truly, I say to you,
you will weep and lament,
while the world rejoices;
you will be filled with sorrow,
but your sorrow will turn into joy."
So it is
with all who give birth
to new hopes,
new dreams,
new visions,
as we shape
a new world order
of equality and love,
of justice and peace,
forever and ever.

—Miriam Therese Winter,
WomanPrayer, WomanSong

REMAIN IN HIM

1 John 2:24-25

Let what you heard from the beginning abide in you. If what you heard from the beginning abides in you, then you will abide in the Son and in the Father. And this is what he has promised us, eternal life.

God's ways, we have long been warned, are simply not our ways. Whatever this universe is about, it is not about anything we think is normal. Who of us would have thought to have made people of different colors? Who of us could have imagined the amoeba? Which one of us would have put stripes on fish and spots on dogs and flowers in deserts? No, God does not think the way we do.

Nor does God expect the same things of us that we too often do of one another. God does not expect perfection, or why would every living thing get an incalculable number of second tries? God does not expect total understanding, or why would life be one long learning process? God does not expect instant acquiescence, or why would there be such a thing as free will? God knows that life is a series of experiences meant to make us better able to handle the next one.

As life goes on, either we get to be more kind, more patient, and less exercised about the little things around us, or, it is apparent, we fail to grow into the ways of the God who is clearly kind, eternally patient, totally confident in the ultimate goodness of this flimsy thing called humanity.

—Joan Chittister, *Songs of Joy*

Prayer

May you walk with God
in the daily unfolding,
in the sharp pain of growing,
in the midst of confusion,
in the bright light of knowing.
May you live in God,
in Her constant compassion,
may yours increase,
in Her infinite wisdom,
in Her passion for peace.
May you walk with God
and live in God
and remain with God
forever.
Amen.

—Miriam Therese Winter,
WomanPrayer, WomanSong

CHOOSE VIRTUE

1 John 2:29—3:1

*If you know that [Jesus Christ] is righteous, you
may be sure that everyone who does right has
been born of him. See what love the Father has
given us, that we should be called children of
God; and that is what we are.*

One evening several years ago I was approaching my
house, returning from a meeting. I slung my purse over my
shoulder and walked to the door, when I suddenly felt a
jerking and pulling at my side. A young man came from
behind me and snatched my purse. Knowing I could not
recover the purse, I yelled at him, "That's wrong. That's
wrong." Later I was amused that, in the midst of anger and
confusion, the moral theology teacher in me came to the fore
and instructed the man about morality.

One does not have to be a moral theologian to say of
some actions, "That's wrong." Most of us have experienced
morally wrong actions and have done our share of them. If
we have not experienced moral wrong ourselves we have but
to watch TV or read the newspapers to see it graphically
displayed. We may find ourselves saying, "That's wrong."
Today's media seem to thrive on publishing the moral
wrongs of individuals: rape, murder, drug abuse, sexual
promiscuity, and marital infidelity. The media also show how

individuals collectively contribute to society's evils through growing poverty and unemployment, cutthroat competition in the marketplace, ruthless individualism, unbridled greed, irresponsibility and infidelity in relationships, declining sexual mores, and business mismanagement.

Powerful though sin is, it does not have the final word. Sin is really powerless in the face of Jesus, the compassionate Lord of all, who shows us how to live a virtuous life. Through the example of Jesus, the grace of the Spirit, and the guidance of the church, we can be strong in the face of evil.

—Elizabeth Willems, *Understanding Catholic Morality*

Prayer

Who shall ascend the hill of the Lord?
And who shall stand in his holy place?
Those who have clean hands and pure hearts,
who do not lift up their souls to what is
false,
and do not swear deceitfully.
They will receive blessing from the Lord,
and vindication from the God of their
salvation.

—Psalm 24:3-5

DO NOT BE DECEIVED

1 John 3:7-8

Little children, let no one deceive you. Everyone who does what is right is righteous, just as [the Son of God] is righteous. Everyone who commits sin is a child of the devil; for the devil has been sinning from the beginning. The Son of God was revealed for this purpose, to destroy the works of the devil.

Even when a woman begins to recognize her longing for God, it can terrify her. She may not want to face her desire for God when it is overwhelmingly unfulfilled. This woman's deep longing is powerful and fearsome precisely because she has known so little fulfillment of longing in her life, knows so well the danger and/or futility of desiring anything for herself, and wearies of the ambivalence that acknowledging her own desires creates for her. Deep longing is painful too when a woman interprets it, generally inaccurately, as a sign that she should continue on a self-denying, self-deprecating path in life. For example, a woman may interpret the sacrament of marriage to mean that she should remain with and submit to an abusive spouse. Facing her desire for God is difficult and painful for a woman precisely because it calls her to see and experience and live her life differently. A woman's desire for the living God undercuts her world.

Given the negative messages that women receive about themselves and their desires and the ambivalence that a powerful experience of longing can evoke in a person, it is easy to understand why many accept the interpretation of women's desire as problematic, if not actively evil. But the consequence to us of holding our desire this way is disastrous.

—Patricia O'Connell Killen, *Finding Our Voices*

Prayer

Our Father, Who art in heaven,
hallowed be Thy name,
Thy kingdom come;
Thy will be done
on earth as it is in heaven.
Give us this day our daily bread;
and forgive us our trespasses,
as we forgive those who trespass against us.
And lead us not into temptation;
but deliver us from evil.
Amen.

LOVE ONE ANOTHER

1 John 3:11, 14-20

For this is the message you have heard from the beginning, that we should love one another. . . . We know that we have passed from death to life because we love one another. Whoever does not love abides in death. All who hate a brother or sister are murderers, and you know that murderers do not have eternal life abiding in them. We know love by this, that [the Son of God] laid down his life for us—and we ought to lay down our lives for one another. How does God's love abide in anyone who has the world's goods and sees a brother or sister in need and yet refuses to help?

Little children, let us love, not in word or speech, but in truth and action. And by this we will know that we are from the truth and will reassure our hearts before him whenever our hearts condemn us; for God is greater than our hearts, and he knows everything.

The relationship between vulnerability, trust, and love is illustrated by the expression "falling in love" with the implication of allowing oneself to be grasped. Is it ironic that we also use the word *fall* negatively to express "a fall from grace" or "the Fall"? Would it be better if we spoke of "falling into grace"?

Love cannot be grasped: one can only be grasped by it, and perhaps in that way the analogy of grace is appropriate. One is surprised by love, but only if one is open to the other, if trust is there. Learning to love is a risky business: we fear rejection, we are afraid to let go, to fall. Yet in that fall lies the only possibility of grace.

—Anne Thurston, *Because of Her Testimony*

Prayer

Author of Love,
You write your law of compassion
    in the Book of Life,
and share with us your longing
for a bond of trust with your people.
Inscribe in our hearts
the story of your saving actions:
that, entering the drama
    of your redemption of the world,
we seek to bring all people
    into unity and peace with You.

—Mary Kathleen Speegle Schmitt,
Seasons of the Feminine Divine

BAPTISM

Mark 1:7-11

[John the Baptist] proclaimed, "The one who is more powerful than I is coming after me; I am not worthy to stoop down and untie the thong of his sandals. I have baptized you with water; but he will baptize you with the Holy Spirit."

In those days Jesus came from Nazareth of Galilee and was baptized by John in the Jordan. And just as he was coming up out of the water, he saw the heavens torn apart and the Spirit descending like a dove on him. And a voice came from heaven, "You are my Son, the Beloved; with you I am well pleased."

Today, we are baptizing our little nephew. He's seven months old, chubby, thoroughly healthy. Ever since we came here for Christmas, I've listened for him in the morning. Like the birds, he begins to sing at first light, and together, they make the most joyous music—the baby, the birds— cooing and calling, as if life depended on it. We've planned the ceremony for late in the afternoon of Epiphany. . . .

The baby's tired and cranky, he has no way of knowing that we are passing through hell. We renounce the forces of evil, and he cries out. As the godmother, I am holding him, and he's fussy, squirming; I have to hold on tight:

Our words wash over you, and you brush them away. The candle catches your eye, your mother's hair and fingers transparent in its light. You want the candle, you want the food your mother has become for you, you want to go down into this night at her breast. Poor little baby, water on your hair, chrism on your forehead, dried milk on your chin. Poor, dear little baby; hold on.

—Kathleen Norris, *The Cloister Walk*

Prayer

Mother of Creation,
in baptism your womb-waters break
  as we are born into new relationship
  with You and your community of faith.
Flood us with the knowledge of your
  mercy and peace:
that your church, embodying your healing
  presence throughout the world,
encourage all humanity into friendship with You.

—Mary Kathleen Speegle Schmitt,
Seasons of the Feminine Divine

ASK AND YOU WILL RECEIVE

1 John 5:14-15

And this is the boldness we have in [the Son of God], that if we ask anything according to his will, he hears us. And if we know that he hears us in whatever we ask, we know that we have obtained the requests made of him.

Our dependence on God's providence is the solid, living faith that God can and will help us. That he can is obvious, because he is almighty; that he will is certain, because he has promised to in many passages of Holy Scripture, and because he is infinitely faithful in all his promises. Christ encourages us to trust these words: "And whatever you ask in prayer, you will receive if you have faith." And the Apostle Peter bids us cast all our cares on the Lord, who cares for us. And why shouldn't God care for us, since he has sent his Son, and with him everything else? St. Augustine says, "How can you doubt that God will do good for you, since he deigned to take our guilt upon us?"

This has to fill us with trust in divine providence, which maintains even the birds and the flowers. But if God feeds the young ravens, which cry to him, and nourishes the birds that neither sow nor reap, how much more will he care for human beings, whom he has made in his own image and whom he has accepted as his children, if we behave as such, following his commandments and trusting him. I don't want our work to become a business; it should remain a work of love. I would wish you to have complete confidence that God will not disappoint us. Take him at his word, and seek first the kingdom of God; and everything else will be granted to you.

—Mother Teresa, *Mother Teresa: Love Stays*

Prayer

Ask, and it will be given you; search, and you will find; knock, and the door will be opened for you. For everyone who asks receives, and everyone who searches finds, and for everyone who knocks, the door will be opened. Is there anyone among you who, if your child asks for bread, will give a stone? Or if the child asks for a fish, will give a snake? If you then, who are evil, know how to give good gifts to your children, how much more will your Father in heaven give good things to those who ask him!

—*Matthew 7:7-11*

BE GUIDED BY THE LIGHT

Isaiah 60:1-6

Arise, shine; for your light has come,
and the glory of the Lord has risen upon
you.
For darkness shall cover the earth,
and thick darkness the peoples;
but the Lord will arise upon you,
and his glory will appear over you.
Nations shall come to your light,
and kings to the brightness of your dawn.
Lift up your eyes and look around;
they all gather together, they come to you;
your sons shall come from far away,
and your daughters shall be carried on their
nurses' arms.
Then you shall see and be radiant;
your heart shall thrill and rejoice,
because the abundance of the sea shall be
brought to you,
the wealth of the nations shall come to you.
A multitude of camels shall cover you,
the young camels of Midian and Ephah;
all those from Sheba shall come.
They shall bring gold and frankincense,
and shall proclaim the praise of the Lord.

The Star Child (A Bedtime Story)

Yes, now it is time for bed. Millions and millions of children are going to sleep. And millions and millions of stars are shining in the sky. Some say the stars are places where love shines through. Some say there is one star for every child and that each time a child is born there is another place where love shines through.

Once upon a time there were a man and a woman to whom was born a baby—a perfectly lovely child like you. This baby's mother and father knew for sure that he was a child of God—a gift from heaven, just like you. And so it happened that his star was very, very bright on the night that he was born. It was so bright I just can't tell you how bright it was!

Still, most people did not notice this bright, bright shining star. They had too much to do to be out looking at stars. They were too busy inside their lighted houses. And it is hard to see the stars when the lights are on, isn't it? Outside in the darkness on the hills were some shepherds. Often they built fires because they were afraid of the dark. But the fires they built were too small for the big darkness.

Otherwise there wasn't much to do out there on the night hills. So the shepherds were always looking up at the shining stars in the dark sky. Of course they saw the bright star of the new baby.

The only other people to see that star were three wise men. They had big houses with lots of lights and all the shiny treasures anyone could ever wish to have. Yet each of them still had one big wish. They wished to find something brighter and better than all the treasures on earth. The wise men saw the star because they were looking for light.

So the only people who saw the star of the baby were some shepherds who had almost nothing and three wise men who had almost everything.

It was such an amazingly bright and beautiful star that the shepherds and wise men all got up and followed it. They walked and walked until finally they were standing right under the star's light. There they saw the star child with his star mother and star father. And suddenly they were filled with love.

Now they could see, too, that the baby was a child of God. And they saw that the light of the wonderful star was love.

In a little while the baby grew up to be as old as you. His name was Jesus. Jesus' mother and father explained to him that he was a child of God. Because he had been told that God was his father, Jesus naturally was very interested in learning about God. He learned everything he could about God from his parents and rabbis, and when he was older he made some important discoveries. He found out that God is love and that everyone is God's child. Jesus saw everyone in the light of God's love. No matter how unfriendly or sick or sad someone seemed to be, he could always see the star child shining through.

Not everyone understood what Jesus was talking about. But those who did lost all their fears, and their good wishes came true, and they were filled with love just like the shepherds and three wise men. Their stars grew very bright.

Because he showed so many people how to let the light of love into their lives, some have called Jesus the Light of the World.

Now let's put everything away and turn off the lights and be very still. Then we can look out the window to see if any bright stars are out tonight—one star for every child of God—one star for you!

—Polly Berrien Berends, *Gently Lead*

Prayer

Light of the world,
we bow before You
in awe and adoration.
Bless us
and our simple faith
seeking understanding.
Epiphany means manifestation,
lifting the veil,
revelation.
Reveal to us then
what we need to know
to love You, and serve You,
and keep Your word
with fidelity and truth,
courage and hope,
this day and always.

—Miriam Therese Winter,
WomanPrayer, WomanSong

ACKNOWLEDGMENTS

We wish to acknowledge the following publishers for permission to reprint previously published material.

From *Because of Her Testimony: The Word in Female Experience* by Anne Thurston. Copyright © 1995 by Anne Thurston. Reprinted by permission of The Crossroad Publishing Company. UK/Commonwealth rights, reprinted by permission of Gill & Macmillan Ltd., Dublin.

From *The Cloister Walk*. Reprinted by permission of Riverhead Books, a division of The Putnam Publishing Group from THE CLOISTER WALK by Kathleen Norris. Copyright © 1996 by Kathleen Norris. UK/Commonwealth rights, reprinted by permission of Janklow & Nesbit.

From *Consider Jesus: Waves of Renewal in Christology* by Elizabeth A. Johnson. Copyright © 1990 by Elizabeth A. Johnson. Reprinted by permission of The Crossroad Publishing Company.

From *Dear Heart, Come Home: The Path of Midlife Spirituality* by Joyce Rupp. Copyright © 1996 by Joyce Rupp. Reprinted by permission of The Crossroad Publishing Company.

From *Finding Our Voices: Women, Wisdom, and Faith* by Patricia O'Connell Killen. Copyright © 1997 by Patricia O'Connell Killen. Reprinted by permission of The Crossroad Publishing Company.

From *Gently Lead: How to Teach Your Children about God While Finding Out for Yourself* by Polly Berrien Berends. Copyright © 1998 by Polly Berrien Berends. Reprinted by permission of The Crossroad Publishing Company.

OF RELATED INTEREST